by Kristi McGee
illustrated by Pam Leavens

Harcourt
SCHOOL PUBLISHERS

Printed in Mexico

ISBN 10: 0-15-350287-8
ISBN 13: 978-0-15-350287-3

Ordering Options
ISBN 10: 0-15-349940-0 (Grade 5 ELL Collection)
ISBN 13: 978-0-15-349940-1 (Grade 5 ELL Collection)
ISBN 10: 0-15-357324-4 (package of 5)
ISBN 13: 978-0-15-357324-8 (package of 5)

2 3 4 5 6 7 8 9 10   126   12 11 10 09 08 07

José's teacher stood up three dominoes, one next to the other. José knew what she was going to do. He and his sister had stood up lines of dominoes like that. José knew what would happen next.

Ms. Gomez tapped the first domino. It fell. It hit the second domino. It fell. That domino hit the last one. Then they were all down.

"This is cause and effect," said Ms. Gomez. "One thing makes another thing happen. Explain what happened."

José raised his hand. "My sister and I do that all the time," he said. "We use more dominoes, though. The first domino fell. It made the second one fall. Then the second one made the third one fall."

"That's exactly right," Ms. Gomez said. "Now
I want you to imagine something. Think of the
first domino as a rainstorm. What happens
when it rains?"

"The plants are watered," Jemma answered.

"Exactly right," said Ms. Gomez. "That's the
second domino. What happens when the plants
are watered?"

Michael raised his hand. "They grow leaves
and flowers," he said.

"That's the third domino," Ms. Gomez replied. Then she drew pictures on the board. She asked the students to describe the connection of the events on the board. José tried. "The flower bloomed because it soaked up the rain from the rainstorm," he said.

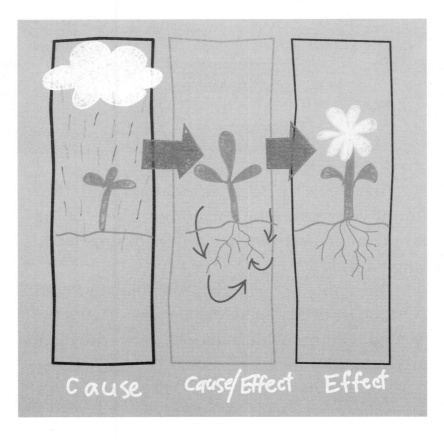

Cause   Cause/Effect   Effect

"Good, José," said Ms. Gomez. "Who can explain it the other way? Start with the rainstorm this time."

Alan raised his hand. "A rainstorm watered the plant, so it grew a flower."

"Yes," said Ms. Gomez. "This is a cause-and-effect relationship. It will help you understand what you read. It will help you to see how things that happen go together. Ask yourself whether one event caused another as you read."

Mike raised his hand. "It's like events in the book *Nothing Ever Happens on 90th Street,*" Mike said. "Eva crumbles her roll and throws it. That causes the birds to come."

"That is right. Who can give another example?" Ms. Gomez asked.

"The ball rolled into the street. It caused the pizza delivery person to have a bike accident," Martina said.

"That is another good example," their teacher said. "Can you think of one more?"

"How about the two characters, Sondra and Mr. Sims, knowing each other?" asked Meg.

"That is different," Ms. Gomez said. The class looked puzzled. "That is a coincidence."

"A what?" José asked.

"A coincidence. That's when things happen at the same time by accident. The events may seem to be connected. However, they really are not," Ms. Gomez explained.

She took out the dominoes again. This time she placed one on the side of her desk. She put the other one on the other side. She shook the desk. The dominoes fell. "See how these dominoes have no direct connection to each other," she said. The class nodded. "They both fell. One didn't cause the other one to fall, though. A coincidence doesn't have a connection. It just seems as if there is a connection."

"Can you please give us a real-life example?" asked Jamal.

"Sure," said Ms. Gomez. "You leave your house without your umbrella. Rain starts to fall. You think, 'If I had my umbrella, it wouldn't have rained.' Really, your not having an umbrella and it raining have nothing to do with each other. What's another example of a coincidence?"

"Another example might be if I bring in a turkey sandwich with lettuce and cranberries for lunch," Sheila said. "My friend also brings a turkey sandwich with lettuce and cranberries on the same day. If we hadn't planned to bring the same kind of lunch, it would be a coincidence."

"That's a good one," said Ms. Gomez. "Now this is your assignment for tomorrow. Write about a cause-and-effect relationship from your life. Then write about a coincidence from your life. Think about the words you use to describe the relationships. *Because, so, then, why*— these words show cause and effect."

José took a long time to walk home. He thought about the assignment. His mother was on the phone. She was looking out the window when he finally reached his apartment.

"I'll get some ideas together. Then I'll ask Mom about them when she is off the phone," he said to himself. He walked to his bedroom and flopped on his bed. Soon he was fast asleep. He didn't wake up until it was almost dark. He smelled something burning.

José jumped off the bed and raced to his door. He saw his mother running down the hall just as he opened the door. She must have smelled the burning odor, too. They ran into each other. Then both of them jumped back.

"Are you okay?" they asked at the same time.

José's mother started laughing first. "You're okay!" she said, in a relieved voice. "I've been calling everyone to find out where you were."

"I got home a long time ago," said José. "However, you were on the phone. I didn't want to interrupt. I decided to lie on my bed and think for a bit. I fell asleep and just woke up to the smell."

"The smell is dinner!" his mother laughed. "I forgot it was in the oven because I was worried about you not being home! I must have checked your room before you got home. Then Grandma called. You must have come in when I was on the phone, talking to Grandma *and* watching the street for you! What a coincidence!"

"Thanks, Mom," said José. "You just helped with my homework!"

Soon José had finished his assignment
based on what had happened earlier. At the end
of the assignment were the words, *Dedicated
to my mother—the Coincidence Queen.* José
decided to honor his mother since she had
helped him with his homework without
knowing it.

José and his mother and sister had the
slightly crusty macaroni and cheese for dinner.
It had been in the oven too long. "I'm sorry
about this cause-and-effect dinner!" José said.
José's mother and sister laughed at his joke.

Scaffolded Language Development

USING CAUSE AND EFFECT WORDS Have students look at these two sentences from pages 6 and 7:

> "The flower bloomed <u>because</u> it soaked up the rain from the rainstorm."
> "A rainstorm watered the plant, <u>so</u> it grew a flower."

Point out that *because* and *so* show causes and effects. *Because* links an effect with its cause. The rainstorm caused the flower to blossom. *So* reverses the order: the cause is followed by the effect. Have students identify the cause and effect in each of the following sentences. Then have them rearrange the sentence using *so* instead of *because*.

1. I was late to dinner because I stayed after school.
2. The macaroni is dry because it cooked too long.
3. We can't go out because we have an assignment to do.
4. I fell asleep because I was tired.

Social Studies

Historical Cause and Effect Have students choose an event from history and find out its cause and the effect it had. Have them fold a piece of paper in half and write about the cause of the event on one half and the effect on the other half. Events might include World War II, Lincoln's assassination, and such.

School-Home Connection

Good Deeds Have students ask a family member to remember a time when they did a good deed. What were the cause and the effect of this deed?

Word Count: 1,019